THE ULTIMATE GUIDE TO
SURFING

JAY MORIARITY & CHRIS GALLAGHER

THE ULTIMATE GUIDE TO
SURFING

JAY MORIARITY & CHRIS GALLAGHER

THE LYONS PRESS

First Lyons Press edition, 2001

First published in the UK 2001
by CollinsWillow
an imprint of HarperCollins*Publishers*
London

Copyright © 2001 by HarperCollins*Publishers*

This book was created by Chilli for HarperCollins*Publishers* Ltd.

1 3 5 7 9 8 6 4 2

ISBN 1-58574-304-6

Color reproduction by Saxon Group

Printed and bound in Italy by Rotolito, Lombarda

The Library of Congress Cataloging-in-Publication Data is available on file.

Edited by: Craig Jarvis. Design by: Chilli/Dakini Ltd.
Photography: Alex Williams & O'Neill/Moller & Hoeffgen;
Front cover: O'Neill/Bill Morris

With thanks to: Matt Warshaw, Ben Marcus — *Surfer* Magazine;
Nick Carrol, Steve Dwyer — *Surfing* Magazine

contents

1   The sport of surfing   12

2   Two sides of the coin   20

3   Getting started   28

4   Basic manoeuvres   44

5   Improving yourself   58

6   Soul surfing: the blurring of the lines   70

7   Surfing big waves   78

8   Surf travel   86

9   Glossary   92

" from the first day **I was hooked.** It felt like I was **floating.** Standing on water..."

"Surfing fits into all categories. It's an ART by the way you can express yourself on a wave. It's a SPORT because you can compete with it, and it's SPIRITUAL because it's just you and Mother Nature. For me it is very spiritual." – **Jay**

"Long lumps of water are generated by winds across the ocean. They gather speed as they approach the shores of the world. When these waves hit shallow spots, the waves pitch and peel towards shore. Really smart animals called 'surfers' have figured out a way to ride these waves with a featherweight plank made of oil, sand and wood. They frolic daily until they are exhausted. They eat, sleep, wake up and do it again and again and again. They can't help themselves." **– Chris**

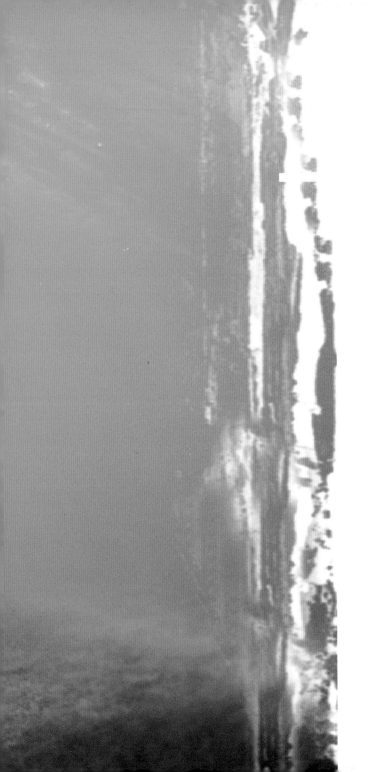

1
the
sport of
surfing

Why do people start surfing? What fires this desire to go out among the breaking waves and try the strangest, but most natural of sports?

It is the simple allure of fun. Surfers are a diverse group of people continually striving to find the adrenaline high that comes from riding large waves or small. It makes them feel good and, as everyone knows, to be happy is an irresistible human condition. Every time we witness somebody tasting it for the first time they show an expression of pure joy, childlike and deeply instinctive. That spontaneous joy is what surfing is all about. It is a very simple equation.

Surfing started out as an activity central to ancient Polynesian society. It was performed by all classes of Hawaiian culture, hundreds of years before Captain Cook happened upon those islands. For them it was a way of communing with the Gods, an arena for showing mastery of their primary element, the ocean, and it was enjoyed for competition, for spectating, for gambling and even courtship.

Left: Toes on the nose.

Opposite Top: The sooner, you're out there, the sooner you can surf! Two surfers scratch for the shoulder.

Cook's major legacy was Christianity and as the years passed the new religion took over the old culture. Surfing became seen as a symptom of heathen laziness, indulgence and, along with gambling, it was outlawed by the colonisers. It wasn't until the early twentieth century that wave-riding gained new acceptance and gradually grew in popularity among Hawaiians and wandering Americans. But this time, it was reborn as a counter-culture activity enjoyed by rebels and people on society's fringes.

The modern pioneers of surfing came from small groups of Hawaiians and Americans who had tapped into a source of profound, healthy gratification while playing very little part in the modern world. They were generally poor, tough people who fished, swam, sailed, paddled and surfed in the ocean and partied, read, sang and created on land. They enjoyed a life of simple pleasures.

However, surfing's golden morning gradually dulled as the years went on, and like a growing thunderstorm on a balmy summer afternoon, the real reasons why we surfed became clouded by the environment we had contrived around our precious pastime. Greed, industry, crowds, aggression – all of these have at times sapped the life forces from surfing to varying degrees. Even today we somehow manage to clutter one of the most unaffected and simple of acts – riding waves.

At schools in California kids can now surf as part of their sports classes. They go training at the beach during school hours and dream of turning pro – an option which emerged in the 1970s and which can now earn a surfer huge amounts of money from sponsors. Professional surfers, like other athletes, are groomed from an early age. Before they hit ten years old many are already out there on a daily basis, learning to compete, training their little bodies, being pushed into bigger surf by their coaches, peers or parents.

Other surfers come to it from different angles. Many will give up more conventional sports, lose their girlfriends, leave their home towns and simply drop their careers in search of a life better suited to performing this profoundly strong encounter with nature.

But these are the two extremes. The joy of surfing is known by all types of people with all types of lifestyle and the call of the water can be heard by anyone – young, old, busy or lazy. Some say we are a tribe, but if we are, our common language is the one pleasure we all share – the simple act of riding a wave. While the non-surfing world has long been fascinated with surfing and recognised that it is indeed something special, only the people who do it, the surfers, understand how deep it really goes.

Opposite Top: In the shaping bay: Chris hard at work building his vehicle.

Opposite: Gliding across a clear face.

Right: A perfect peak confronts a lone surfer.

The dawn glide

The promise of a new swell means excitement and expectation. You get up when it's still dark, quickly wolf down some fruit for instant, pure energy and, as fast as you can, you get yourself to the beach. Down there it is cold, the beach is empty. But the water is warm or at least somehow inviting. It is a perfect honey-coloured dawn and you can almost feel the glow pulsing off the shoreline. There is a slight breeze, ever so light and blowing from the land out to sea. A short wetsuit is all you need – short legs and short arms. It is flexible and it keeps the breeze off. You zip it up, and bounce around on the sand in your bare feet. You're getting ready, mentally and physically, and though you may still feel sleepy and half of you wishes you were still in your bed, you know the first rush of water will wash it all away. The sun is slowly appearing over the edge of the sea and golden reflections light the cresting waves. Wax. You need some wax. An ecstasy of fumbling as you scrabble desperately through your bag. The waves are looking so good, and there's still no one around. You can't do it fast enough; you just want to be out there. A few brisk rubs with the wax and your board is primed.

Left: Through dawn's early light.

Opposite: We just call it fun...

Time to warm up. A few more bounces, stretching your leg and arm muscles. You loosen your shoulders, then a quick sprint down to the water's edge.

You splash out through the inside waves, walking in the shallows, then jump under a broken wave. It clears away all other thoughts and you feel the comfort of your natural element. You spring onto your board and start to paddle. Energy pours through your arms and hands and emanates from your fingertips as you stroke outside. You duck-dive a big wall of whitewater and then another and another, and soon enough, you're out where all is calm and peaceful. Your heart beats strongly, your breathing is still quick from the mild exertion of paddling and duck-diving. You are alone behind the perfect, curling waves as the sun starts its rise into a clear azure sky. Before you the day stretches out full of promise, beauty and liquid wonder.

A set of waves approaches. You let the first one slip beneath you, feeling the familiar energy as it passes below. The second one looks good. You turn and start paddling towards the beach like you have so many times before. You can feel the wave push and lift underneath you and, at the instant when you catch it, when your board and the wave reach the same speed, you jump to your feet and glide down the face of this glassy, stretching, arcing wall of water. You fly with it, feeling its energy through the soles of your feet and as the moments flash by in a blur of vivid colour, you know once again why you've decided you'll surf forever.

...Spiritual activity, sport, art form. Whatever you want to call it. We just call it fun.

" the promise of a new swell means excitement and expectation "

2
two sides
of the coin

"It's like if you imagine flying on a cloud. You're totally free and you're going really fast. You can do whatever you want, you feel light, your mind is clear and you just go with it. I surf because I love to surf. I love being around the ocean and in the water. Surfing is one of the most pure and exciting ways to enjoy the ocean's power." **– Jay**

"When I was a kid I played every sport under the sun. I chose surfing because it is the hardest sport in the world to master. It is an endless journey of improvement and oceanic mastery. Surfing satisfies my manic need for activity." **– Chris**

Sometimes it is hard to believe that a mere surfboard is responsible for transporting so many people to such far-flung and diverse corners of our planet and to so many unexplored alcoves of the soul. It is astounding that people can experience so much pleasure, by simply riding pulses of nature's energy on a craft made of foam and fibreglass.

One thing is for sure – surfers are strange beings. Like frantic phantoms we perform quirky, obscure daily rituals, exiting on whims and returning when our own arcane schedule dictates. We live by an agenda totally obscure to rational mortals yet so clear to other surfers. Ours is a schedule revolving around the tides, the phases of the moon, wind directions and responsibilities. Shuffling and reprioritising life's duties comes naturally to us. The goal is simple – to make time for surf.

Yet, in our lifelong pursuit of this irresistible activity, are we surfers simply a group of hedonists whose stoked fire threatens to burn all that we love? Or are we an enlightened tribe who have been allowed a glimpse of the void, and discovered an alternative to the quiet desperation of daily life?

Despite the forward thrust of modern surfing – in technology, marketing and all-round extremity – it has managed to maintain an almost mystical aspect to it. It's hard for non-surfers to understand but for us there is something extraordinarily powerful, a truly deep-rooted stimulus that keeps calling us back to the sea. We'll keep going back even when it is teeming with fellow surfers or when the water is cold, lonely and windy, with the barking seals, squawking gulls and unseen threats from below as our only company. At times we wonder if we control surfing, or if surfing controls us because something unusual keeps us stoked. It keeps us coming back for more, through injuries and cold winters, through flat spells and giant storms. Through the joy and frustration we continually return to the ever-changing, fluid classroom – the sea in all her moods.

As more and more people begin to realise what a healthy pursuit surfing is, so more people get involved and start on the learning curve. That means more happy

Opposite: Spectators delight at the solitary surfer.

Right: Mindsurfing.

people, but it also means, more surfers. Things have reached a critical stage around many urban areas, where some of the surf spots are now truly dysfunctional. Overcrowding in the line-up often leads to incidents of aggression and increasingly dangerous situations. Sometimes only jungle laws apply. The primary predators do what they want in the surf, while the lower forms of life – non-locals, beginners, 'kooks', bodyboarders etc. – have to scavenge what they can and try hard to avoid the gnashing teeth of the aggressors.

But it doesn't need to be like this. The wise surfer realises that it's a big old world out there and there are many undiscovered line-ups waiting to be found. It's all about aspiration. If you really want to surf uncrowded waves there are scores of realistic options. You may have to travel long and hard to far-off lands. Or it might be found in your own backyard, in among the pack at your crowded homebreak. The destination is a state of mind.

So no-one knows for sure whether it is blind self-indulgence or enlightened mystical wisdom. But we do know that the sensations are addictive and profound. We surf for the feelings that come when you're gliding across the water and the wave is roaring behind you. When you paddle into a big wave, as you look down, it's like leaning over the edge of a multi-storey building, and the only route out is to jump to your feet and fly down this moving mountain of liquid.

Opposite: Who's going to get the last set?

Above: Who's out there?

Right: An amusement for misspent youth.

25

Sometimes when a wave catches you it is so big and so frightening that it brings you out in a primeval fear, a terror that only a few people ever experience. But those moments are worth it. Thinking you're going to die is life's flipside of feeling like you can fly.

But as well as the horrors, there are unimaginable moments that surely transcend self-indulgence. How can you fault experiences like sitting among schools of millions of teeming fish; feeling the force from giant whales belly-flopping nearby and smelling their sprayed breath in the air; surfing with dolphins; watching the sun rise and set and its endless effects on the colours of water? You can't argue against being fit and healthy, tired and sore from a day of surfing thick, grinding waves, your eyelids caked with salt crystals, the glowing phosphorescence following your tiny boat as you cruise back to camp in the hot tropics, and knowing that if the world were to end today you would leave this plane of existence a very happy person.

To surf is to be lucky.

Opposite: Santa Cruz sunset.

Above: Locked in.

Right: Board repairs can be fun.

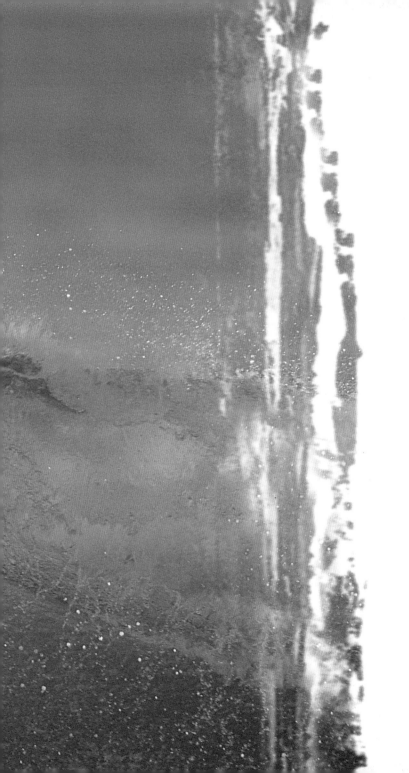

3
getting started

"My best moment when I first started surfing was the day I actually stood up and rode a wave on my feet. It seemed like it was taking me forever to actually stand up, but once I did I went nuts. I was so stoked! Everything I had been working on finally happened and I was just hooked." **– Jay**

"I wasn't exactly a beginner, but when I was about 12 the three-fin surfboard was invented. This made all the places on a wave accessible. Where a twin-fin dared not go, the thruster went with speed and commitment. For about six months I couldn't sleep at night thinking about tomorrow's six-hour session." **– Chris**

" the joy of surfing is known by all types of people "

For any relationship to be long lasting, it is the early days that are the most important. So it is with surfing. The best way of getting to know the sea in its many moods is to swim in it, get used to the power. Get familiar with breaking swells, and learn to accept that ultimately the sea is in complete control. It thus deserves respect. But you will also learn, gradually, what is dangerous and what is not. For instance, most people think that being tumbled by a breaking wave is necessarily painful. It can be, but nine times out of ten it is a quick, high energy, but painless experience. Overcome such basic fears by watching others and trying for yourself. Learn the parameters. It is in this simple way that a surfer begins the relationship that for many lasts forever.

Surfboards

Your surfboard is by far the most important piece of equipment you need.

It is your steed, your means to an end, your best friend. The choice of possible surfboards is endless. The board that will work for you as an individual generally depends on three main factors:

1. Your build.
2. The type of waves that you habitually surf.
3. Your grade of skill/years of experience.

Surfers can become obsessive about boards and find they need different ones for subtly different conditions. Like Eskimos describing snow, there are so many variables when it comes to breaking waves that the need for a selection of different boards, called a 'quiver', becomes necessary. But to begin with one should be quite enough.

Just as you wouldn't learn to drive in a Formula One car, you shouldn't start surfing on a board finely tuned for a professional. In general, a novice should begin on a wider, thicker, more full-shaped surfboard than someone of experience would ride. These factors allow for more stability and better paddling ability. More paddle-power means more waves caught, which means a quicker learning curve. A surfboard should float a surfer easily but should be neither too cumbersome nor too loose. A good basic rule is for a beginner's board to be a few feet longer than he/she is.

Once you have become proficient and worked out which sorts of waves you prefer then you can start being more selective with boards. You will need a different board for bigger waves (generally longer and more spear-shaped), smaller waves (generally smaller with numerous shape options), waves that break quickly over shallow reef (again, more spear-shaped), or waves that break gently over sloping sand bottoms (longer and wider with more overall volume).

And should you want to tackle the giant waves of Mavericks or the moving mountains of Hawaii, then it becomes a whole new ball game (tip: you'll need a Rhino-chaser).

Wetsuits

These are less complicated which is good because most surfers spend more surf time encased in rubber than not. When the waves are good there could be any number of factors that make some sort of wetsuit necessary – there might be a chilly offshore wind, or a distinct lack of sun, or even a freezing current. These days with the incredible advances of wetsuit technology people are surfing in Alaska and around the polar caps with minimal discomfort. A couple of millimetres of rubber, which used to be so cumbersome in the past, are now just barely noticeable. Most people agree that surfing in boardshorts under a blazing sun is the ideal, but unfortunately the geography of our planet won't allow this for everyone.

It has been proven that up to half of a human's body heat can be lost through the head, so in cold water a hood is imperative. Your extremities – fingers and toes – get coldest first, so boots and gloves are also useful. It is no good surfing if your feet are so cold that you can't feel your board underneath you.

In warmer conditions a thin wetsuit can be worn for protection against the sun and minor brushes with the reef, or as a means of combating the wind-chill factor. It is easy to find a good suit. Just shop around before you buy – in general, the stretchier it is, the better. In the coldest water, surfers use 5 or 6 millimetre wetsuits.

Accessories

Along with the wetsuit another piece of equipment often overlooked is the helmet. Many surfers consider them superfluous but a helmet provides protection from hard coral reefs, from a flying board and from cold wind or hot sun. Some people swear by them, others never wear them. It largely depends on your level of skill, the waves you surf and of course, how much value you place on looking cool.

Opposite: A beachbreak wave is the most user-friendly.

Above: Your leash should be secure – it is your lifeline.

Below: Soft-edge fins provide major protection.

"ultimately, the sea is in complete control. for any relationship to be long-lasting, it is the early days that are most important"

You will also need a couple of leashes to stop your board from being washed away every time you fall (don't worry, everyone does it, even the experts). Before leashes were invented, a wipe-out meant you had a long swim to the beach where you often found your board damaged on the rocks. Nowadays a simple urethane leash attached from the board's tail to the surfer's ankle prevents this. There are a couple of types of leashes, the basic difference being some leashes are made for big waves, and have a higher breaking strain but due to their larger size and thickness result in more drag. The small wave leash is thinner and has less drag, but is not as strong and will break easily in bigger surf.

These days, with more and more surfers paddling out into immense, hazardous conditions, a board securely attached to the ankle can sometimes actually be more of a liability. Thus the quick-release leash has come to the fore – one can simply pull the pin and the board will be released.

The finish on a new surfboard is an extremely slick, shiny and slippery surface. Traction pads or wax are used to stop a surfer from slipping. Once you've waxed your board a few times, a wax comb can be used. Running it over the wax once or twice, making a grid pattern, will greatly increase the effectiveness of the wax, and will save on the amount of wax you go through.

The surf

There are many types of waves. Some are large and dangerous, others are gentle, mellow and ideal for learners. It is imperative that you find a suitable wave to start on, one that you are confident you can deal with. To be out of your depth in big surf is just plain dangerous. It should be avoided at all cost.

A gentle, rolling beachbreak is perfect for beginners. Ask someone who knows and, ideally, once you have found a safe place to learn, go out with someone of experience who can guide you around the break. Even before paddling out, always assess the conditions and see if you think you are up to it. You may not truly know your limits yet, but if you are not confident, then just wait and watch from the beach. Always seek advice from lifeguards or

Right: A perfect peak.

Opposite: Bottom turning for a lone spectator.

experienced surfers. Experts, you will find, rarely mind helping beginners because they've all been there themselves.

Wave types

Unlike other sports, your playing field is constantly changing. Waves are created by a combination of tides, wind and storms far out to sea. How these waves reveal themselves at your local break is determined by a number of factors. Wave types can be broadly described by a number of general types:

1. Beachbreak waves break over a sand bottom and, since the sand is constantly shifting, they are usually less predictable than reefs or pointbreaks. However, with fewer hazards like coral or rocks, beachbreaks are generally fun to ride and more suitable for novices.

2. Pointbreak waves occur around a headland where there is a bend in the coast. These tend to be the best waves for surfers, since points have the potential to create long, unvarying waves. One of the world's best pointbreaks is a spot called Jeffrey's Bay in South Africa, where surfers have been known to ride fast, clean waves for almost a mile in length. They can break over sand, but generally crash onto rocks or coral reefs. Most are for experts only,

but if you find a gentle pointbreak that is safe to learn on, then go for it. It will allow you to ride longer waves, which will help your surfing immeasurably.

3. Reefbreaks are generally regarded as the most dangerous type of wave to surf. They break over rocks or coral shelves which, since they don't move around like sand does, tend to make the waves break in a more uniform shape and in roughly the same place. This is ideal for lining up and finding a good take-off spot. Like all waves, reefbreaks vary in shape and size, and not all of them are extremely dangerous. However, the world's best reefbreaks are, which makes them more exciting to watch or to ride. Generally it would be advised for beginners to avoid reefbreaks at first, until they are confident and proficient.

There are dozens of other types of wave and endless ways, both useful and contrived, to describe them, but those are the basic types. The ocean bottom's gradient, or shelf, is also important to the way a wave breaks. A gentle incline of the seabed makes for softer, gentle rollers, while a sharp change from deep to extremely shallow water usually makes for a surging beast of a wave, like Pipeline in Hawaii or Teahupoo in Tahiti.

Here are some more descriptions of waves that you might hear mentioned and are useful to know:

1. Close-outs – these are bad, unwanted waves. They break all at once in a long line, allowing surfers nowhere to go except straight towards the shore. Surfers try to avoid taking off on close-outs and beginners should learn to recognise them and not waste their energy trying to catch them.

2. Reforms – these are waves that initially break over a shallow bottom, then back off as they pass through deep water, then break again closer to shore. Reforms occur when a deep gully lies between two shallow sandbars or reefs. Reforms can be fun to surf and are sometimes ideal for learners.

3. Double-ups – these occur when one swell catches up with another and forms a thicker, steeper wave breaking close to the shore. These waves are powerful and unpredictable. Some experienced surfers enjoy the thrill of trying to read and anticipate the erratic action of a double-up. Most people avoid them because they are likely to break boards or limbs. Beginners should be kept away from double-ups at all costs.

Currents also play a significant part in affecting the surf. They have the potential to be extremely dangerous but once you understand the basic mechanisms of a

Right: Just below the surface lurks a menacing reef.

Opposite: A Santa Cruz pointbreak.

current they become easier to deal with, and can be used to great advantage.

1. Rip currents – these are hazardous to surfers and swimmers alike. Most lifeguard rescues are performed on swimmers who are caught in rips. When broken waves wash towards the shore they carry a large volume of water with them. After the wave energy is spent, this water will naturally find a way back out to sea, and it is this movement that forms a rip. Rips are usually simple to spot – they look like a river flowing through the calmer water and they often have foam and debris flowing with them. If you are caught in a rip, paddle or swim at a right angle to the current, and you will escape it. Do not try and paddle against the current – it will tire you out quickly – simply move across it to calmer water nearby.

Although dangerous to swimmers and those who are not wise to them, rips can be useful for surfers wanting a quick and easy paddle out to the line-up. Learn where the rips go and how to use them to your advantage.

2. Cross-currents – these move up or down the beach, parallel to shore. They can be extremely strong in surf zones and have the potential to wash you a long way from your original paddle-out spot. These too can be hazardous if the current is washing directly towards a pier or a rock outcrop. If you find yourself stuck in a cross-current, the best thing to do is to catch the whitewater of a broken wave and paddle towards shore on your board, then re-assess your approach from the safety of the beach.

If there are lifeguards and you are unsure about the conditions, it is always a good idea to ask for advice.

Tides

They can make all the difference. A low tide can expose rocks or reef, or cause the waves to back off and weaken. At other places the waves might actually stop breaking on higher tides as the water fills up over sandbars. High tides can also cause backwash, when the water rebounds off rocks or sandbanks and flows back out to sea against the waves. This can disturb the incoming waves to such an extent that they become unrideable.

Surf schools

When committing yourself to surfing, it is advisable to join a surf school for a while, just to learn the basics. Certified surf instructors are well trained and their aim is the same as yours – to get you surfing. Surf schools haven't been around for that long, and many experienced surfers never had the chance to use one. So if you're learning now you should take advantage of their experience. It can speed up the learning process enormously.

Here is what they will teach you in a practical manner:

Paddling

When you paddle for a wave you need to be centred over the board and feel comfortable and balanced on it. At first it will be hard to find a stable position but over time it will start to come naturally. The board needs to be flat on the water, with no water covering the nose area – if there is, it means you are too far forward. Similarly, if the nose is pointing towards the sky and wiggling about with your every move, then you are lying too far back. By lying over the centre of the board you are in the optimum position to get the most speed out of paddling.

Keep your head up, your buttocks clenched and your chest tight. This will give you more leverage from your paddling movements. Extend your legs, put your knees close together and try to rest them on the board. Do not let your legs or feet hang over the edges of your board – this will hinder your forward movement.

Cup your hands and with each alternate paddle stroke, stretch as far forward as you can then scoop the water, trying to literally pull yourself forward through it. At this stage only your arms and your shoulders are moving while the rest of your body rests on the board. This way you will minimise energy wastage – you will find that paddling, at first, can be exhausting.

Catching waves

"Surfing is an incredibly selfish thing. What else can you call something that involves sitting there and looking at the horizon for half of your life?" (Former top Australian surfer, Terry Fitzgerald)

He's right. While waiting for a wave your focus should always be on the horizon since this tells you what is coming and helps you avoid being surprised by bigger waves. Once you have found a position in the line-up that is both safe and near enough to the cresting waves to try taking off, the best thing to do is to mark the spot with reference points on the land. Find a chimney, a tree or a rock – anything that doesn't move – and then find another in a different direction. With two points of reference you should be able to maintain your position. Hopefully, when a wave approaches, you should be in the correct place to catch it. With a wave approaching, sit up on your board, grab a rail, kick and paddle with a sideways movement to turn around. Timing is very important here. Start paddling just before the wave reaches you and as it is about to peak. After just a few strokes you should feel the force of the wave beneath you. When you sense it lifting you up and pushing you forward, paddle hard. Don't stop paddling too early because the wave pulse could still just sweep underneath you. Through a mixture of hard paddling and even kicking your feet, you should be able to get into the wave and tap into its speed. Then try standing up.

Standing up

As soon as you can feel that you have caught the wave, prepare for the flick-up. The basic protocol of the flick-up may seem like a laboured exercise, but once learned, it gets easier and quicker.

Place your hands flat on the deck of your board as if you're about to do a press-up. Your hands should be fairly wide apart, and most definitely should not be wrapped around the rails.

Arch your back as you push down with your hands, and swing your feet up underneath you in one smooth motion. This movement is similar to a squat-thrust exercise and it is worth practising at home on the floor. Look ahead of you, to where you want to go on the wave. Your stance should be fairly wide for stability – a little wider than your shoulders at most –

Below: (Left to right) Paddle and take-off – there are two forces at play when you stand up, the forward speed of the wave and the force of gravity on you the surfer.

but not too wide. Your knees should be bent a little and your front foot should be centred over the stringer. Your back foot should be planted sideways over the tail of your board. Spread your arms to aid balance. Put your best foot forward, whichever feels natural, and proceed to ride the wave.

In all these processes remember to relax. If you are tense and nervous then your body will be stiff and easily thrown off balance. You will fall, many times, but don't read this as a sign of failure. Everyone falls and every wipe-out is a lesson learned. Remember that no matter how hard it seems at first, you are in the process of learning something magical. The key, you will find on all levels, is to go with it.

The unwritten rules

It is here worth mentioning the rules. There are none, only a set of unwritten codes which everyone is expected to abide by. They are there to enhance your safety and your enjoyment of riding waves.

First there is the 'drop-in' rule. If a surfer is up and riding on a wave then that surfer should be left alone to ride unimpeded. When two people are paddling for the same wave it is the one closer to the breaking part who has the right of way. If a surfer were to take off on the same wave and impede the first surfer's ride, that would be deemed unacceptable (a 'drop-in').

For the surfer starting out, the best rule to remember is that if someone is paddling for a wave with the intent of catching it, or has already caught it and is up and riding, then leave that one well alone. Obey this simple rule and there shouldn't be any problems.

Also, when paddling out, it is your duty to avoid the person surfing – they have enough to worry about already. If this

means that you have to paddle into the whitewater and get hammered, then you still have to do it.

It is important to note that many beaches these days have surfing/bathing areas clearly demarcated. This is to protect the bathers from being hurt by surfboards and is the sort of common sense rule that shouldn't be ignored.

Above: Gliding along a smooth, early morning wall.

A buddy system – surfing with another person – is also a good idea when you start surfing. Learning with someone else means that not only can you push each other and help each other improve, but you also make things safer. If something goes wrong, it's good to know there's someone who can help.

Finally don't forget the sharks. They are out there, in almost all surf areas of the world, and are another good reason not to surf alone. It cuts down the risks when you are trespassing in the food chain. The shark rules are that you should avoid dawn or dusk surfs, rivermouths and dirty water. Sharks don't usually bite surfers deliberately but they do attack them nonetheless. If you feel scared, get out or get over it.

4
basic
manoeuvres

All good surfing is built on these crucial building blocks:

1. The bottom turn.
2. The top turn.
3. The cutback.
4. The tuberide.

Firstly, before we get into these moves, here is a brief description of a major style difference that you may by now have picked up on.

Backhand and forehand surfing

These are the two surfing stances. If you surf with your left foot forward you are a known as a 'regular-foot', and with your right foot forward you are a 'goofy-foot'. Which one you are depends on your natural instinct when standing on a board. A good way to find this out is to try riding a skateboard. Whichever way feels best (right foot at the front or left foot at the front) will most likely be the way you will ride a surfboard.

It makes a difference in the surf because waves break in two directions – running to the left or towards the right, from the point-of-view of the riding surfer. So, if you were on a right-breaking wave and were a natural-footer (left foot forward) you would be facing the wave. You would be surfing 'forehand'.

If, on the other hand, at the same break you had your right foot forward you would be surfing with your back to the breaking part of the wave. This is 'backhand' surfing. In general forehand is the easier position to learn on, but soon enough you will be riding lefts or rights and developing different skills for each.

The bottom turn

A bottom turn sets up all your speed for the wave. There are two forms of this basic turn – a forehand bottom turn and a backhand bottom turn.

The forehand bottom turn

Let's take it from the position of the rider who has caught a wave and got to their feet. You will have felt the power of the wave rising underneath and will have already negotiated an initial drop down its face. When you get to the bottom of the wave, gently apply pressure on the inside rail with your toes, with slightly more pressure coming from your back foot. Your knees should be bent thus storing energy that can be released as you turn. Your front foot is used to guide you and counterbalance the weight applied by your

Opposite: Jay gouging through morning glass.

Above: Fish-eye view.

back foot, which controls your turn. Again this can be practised on land on a skateboard. Ride along on a flat surface and simply lean over to turn yourself. After a few tries and scraped knees you will gain sensitive control over your weight distribution and find you can carve smooth, flowing turns. There is very little difference when you are on a surfboard. Remember that the bottom turn sets your speed and angle for the next part of the wave, so mastery of this basic move helps in everything to come ahead.

The backhand bottom turn

At first this feels more difficult than the forehand turn, but it is essentially the same movement using your heels instead of your toes to weight the inside rail.
Take off and when you get to the bottom of the wave, gently apply pressure on the inside rail with your heels. Too much pressure could result in the tail popping out, and too little pressure could result in a weaker turn, less speed and more chance of being caught by the wave's falling lip. Instead of concentrating too much on the

Above: With outrageous manoeuvres becoming the norm, more and more surfers are taking to the sky.

mechanisms of the turn, look over your leading shoulder and set your sights on a particular part of the wave where you want to get to. As always, remember to allow instinct and feel to play a part in this learning process.

" a **bottom turn** sets up all your speed for the **wave** "

The top turn
The forehand top turn

The top turn is done, as the name implies, off the top of the wave using the speed generated from the bottom turn. It is a useful move for both using up speed and gaining more. Carving a smooth arc from the base of the wave to the top also, you will find, feels good.

From the initial bottom turn look ahead to spot a point at the top of the wave where you want to turn. Apply pressure to your back foot, which should be centred over the board, and use your front foot to direct the turn. Arms play a vital part for balance here.

With your board heading for the top of the wave at an angle, apply pressure with your toes to your inside rail. When you reach the zenith of your turn unweight your board and then apply immediate pressure to the opposite (outside) rail as you turn off the top. This will angle you back down the face of the wave. You'll get a boost of speed as you drop down the face again and set up your next move.

The backhand top turn

Once again, in essence it is the same move as a forehand top turn, except with your back to the wave. The main difference is your restricted view of the wave.
As you ease off the bottom your weight

Below: (Left to right) A classic backhand bottom turn, top turn combination performed by Chris, clearly showing how the surfer should flow with the wave and utilise the energy and speed provided by the wave instead of opposing it.

49

should once again be on your inside rail, applied through your heels. As you lay into the turn your view over your leading shoulder will reveal a point on the wave where you want to bank. As you head up the wave towards this point, your weight should be centred over the board with no real pressure over either rail. At the top of the wave, transfer your weight back to the original outside rail by applying force through your toes. Open your shoulders and pivot your torso. Use your back foot to stabilise any sliding or erratic movements of the board – keep it smooth. All being well you should now be heading back down the wave face and still have plenty of speed for your next bottom turn.

The cutback
The forehand cutback

A cutback is a sharp change of direction on the open wave face, back towards the curl, with the aim of returning you to the most powerful part of the wave. Before shifting your weight from your inside to the outside rail, twist your head and shoulders around in the direction you intend to turn. Your leading shoulder will automatically point towards your target. Ease into the turn by applying gentle pressure on your back foot and inside rail. Your arc will bring you back towards the breaking part of the wave. You are now in effect riding backhand. As you approach the foam, once again re-apply pressure to your outside rail, and prepare to bank off the whitewater. As you hit the foam everything will feel light under your feet but you need to keep your turn going regardless. Momentum will bring you around.

Once you bounce off the foam, the wave basically does the rest of the work for you. The wave should push your board back under your body, and you should emerge with excess speed, which you can use for your next turn.

Opposite: Chris doing a powerful turn off the top of a thick left in Santa Cruz.

Below: Surfing is as fun to do as it is to watch.

" remember to allow **instinct** and feel to play a part in the **learning process** "

The backhand cutback

With your back to the wave, you are basically making the same turn as above. Shift your weight onto the outside rail and drive the board back around towards the foam. As you approach the foam your weight should be shifting back again, onto your inside rail so that when you hit the foam your weight is balanced. Remember to watch the foam where you want to hit it.

When you bank off the foam, prepare for landing by keeping your knees bent and your weight centred over the board.

The Tuberide
Forehand tuberides

Riding in the tube is by far the most frightening and exhilarating part of surfing. One top surfer in the 1970s, Shaun Thomson, summed up its indescribable

delights by saying that "time slows down in the tube." Certainly the senses are heightened in the extreme and the surfer relies almost entirely on instinct as the roaring chaos of a breaking wave explodes all around. The promise of experiencing a deep tuberide is a good enough reason in itself to learn how to surf.

For good tubes, known as 'hollow' waves, a complex set of conditions needs to be in place. Tubes can appear at any beach though, and one characteristic of good, experienced surfers is that they always seem to find tuberides, no matter what the conditions. The truths is, tubes, or 'barrels', are hard to predict and the more experience you have, the sharper your eye for a hollow section.

Bigger days, lower tides and offshore winds all increase your chances of finding tubing waves. The more size there is, the

more force the waves will break with and if the water is shallow the waves will break harder still. Offshore winds hold up the wave faces and keep the swell from breaking until it reaches very shallow water. The shallower the water, the better shaped the tube will be.

While riding, look out for a section that might get hollow. As this part of the wave begins to stand up in front of you, control your speed and positioning with subtle turns to leave yourself in the pocket. You can do this by applying pressure with your back foot; stalling the board to slow yourself into a more suitable position. Hands dragged in the wave face also slow you down. The deeper you dig your arm into the wall of water, the slower you go.

Get low on your board with your weight towards the back, then let the inside rail and fins steer the board up the face a little

Above: The limits to what can be done on the medium of a moving canvas have yet to be found.

Below: (Left to right) The backhand cutback is a timeless move with ultimate function which when performed correctly as in this sequence of Chris, is a beautiful and fluid movement.

as the wave pitches out in front of you. This rise in height will increase your speed. Don't get a fright when you find yourself inside the spinning cavern. With the noise, speed and proximity to power, many people become disorientated and assume they are about to fall, which they usually then do. If you stay calm and carry on riding just as you were, there's every chance you'll make it out.

The worst thing you can do is panic inside the tube and try to either straighten out or pull through the top. Just sit back and enjoy the view. Remember to watch for chunks of falling lip. If you do fall you might be able to dive through the face, but it's more likely that you won't have a chance. Try to kick your board away from yourself as you go. Be frightened but bear in mind what former World Champion and one of the best tuberiders of all time, Shaun Thomson, also said "deep inside the tube is probably the safest place to wipe-out."

Left: Sometimes the result of trying to be too radical is a broken board. Matt Archbold, Hawaii.

Opposite: Chris fully committed and looking for a way out of this tight little barrel.

The backside tuberide

For a long time this move was classified as technically difficult. Nowadays it seems pretty easy. Just follow a few simple procedures and the backhand tuberide is another simple yet addictive skill to have under your belt.

As the hollow part of the wave stands up for you, you need to drop your back knee and grab your outside rail for stabilisation. This will bring you down really low onto your board and in a good position to see what is happening ahead. Then, once you have visualised a line to take through the tube you need to square your shoulders to the wave. This will put you on a strong and clean drive through the barrel. Keep the line, even if you can't see anything, you'll be surprised how solid this stance is.

If you're able to ride in the tube backhand without holding your rail at all, you don't need to be reading this.

" time slows down in the tube "

Overleaf: Jay performs a flawless roundhouse cutback, showing in exquisite detail the subtle weight changes and shoulder movements, as well as showing the reason for the cutback: to get back to the power source of the wave.

5
improving
yourself

"When Occy first came on the scene in 84-85, I would do anything it took to get videos of him. I would study his technique on slo-mo. When it finally clicked and I carried it over to the surf it was like a snowball of improvement. To this day those techniques I learned are the basis of my surfing." – **Chris**

After you have mastered the four basic manoeuvres, your level of improvement will naturally lead you to try more advanced moves. Think about trying some of these:

1. The Floater
2. The Tailslide
3. The Aerial

"I remember the day I did my first floater. It just felt like a huge progression. I knew that day I was hooked on radical moves" – Jay

The floater

More difficult than it looks, the floater is a move in which you use your lateral speed to climb onto and over a breaking section. As a section of the wave breaks in front of you, use all the speed you have and project the board onto the lip. Instead of the usual straight up, straight down movement of an off-the-lip turn, you literally 'float' along the whitewater, before dropping down to the base of the wave again. Remember to unweight as you ride along the broken foam. Keep your weight centred and your legs bent while floating – this lowers your centre of gravity.

Watch for a smooth, clean landing point and keep an eye on the front edges of your board to try and avoid digging one of your rails in. Landing is probably the trickiest part, particularly on a wave that has hollowed out beneath you. A gentle touch is needed, often helped by foam bouncing upwards underneath your board and cushioning the landing.

Opposite: When doing a big floater, remember to watch for a clean landing point.

Above: The tail-slide is a new school manoeuvre. Many old school power surfers scoff at this turn, saying that is a trick utilising no power, but there is no denying the fact that a perfectly executed tail-slide like this one is a satisfying move to watch, and an ultra-radical turn to pull off.

The tail-slide

A new school manoeuvre, the tail-slide has come from being basically a mistake or an indication of poor surfing, into a functional part of modern high-performance riding. It requires a fair amount of power to be applied to the turn, and a complete unweighting of the tail area.

Surfing fast down the line of a wave, gear up for a cutback. While making the first direction change, instead of digging your fins in and jamming the turn, take your weight completely off the fins mid-turn. This should result in the fins popping slightly out, and the tail sliding because there is less bite. Your foot, centred over the tail, should still have a semblance of control over the tail area as you actually end up virtually surfing backwards, or fin first, for a moment. Your front foot comes into play as the main balancing point. You can regain control of the tail by applying

pressure once you have completed the turn and want to continue with the wave.

The aerial

This is the turn that revolutionised surfing, as we know it. First performed in the 1980s by surfers like Martin Potter and Christian Fletcher, the aerial turn was ignored and even scorned until fairly recently. It is the most difficult move to do properly, but it can be extremely satisfying. It is a move of split-second timing and it needs a lot of practice. There will be many failed aerial attempts before you pull off a really good one. But keep flying, don't be discouraged. An aerial is essentially an off-the-lip, projected into the air. Speed is the most important factor in this move, along with the right type of wave. As you bank off the top of the wave, instead of allowing the lip to send you back onto the wave face, project your board out,

Left & Opposite: The aerial is
basically an off-the-lip... projected
into the air.

one digging in if you land awkwardly. Look for a good point of landing and don't bottle out whilst in the air. Follow through with the turn and you could be achieving the impossible!

Apart from learning advanced moves, there are many more aspects involved in improving as a surfer, and it's a combination of all of them that will make you surf better.

off the top of the wave and into the air. Many surfers hold onto the rails at this stage, to keep their board and feet connected. At other times surfers will 'ollie' the board as they hit the lip, a skateboard move that allows you to pop the board upwards underneath your feet. Remember to keep your back foot centred, and to unweight on take-off. Whilst in the air try and switch your weight to be completely centred over the board. The important thing is to stay with the board's trajectory. Watch your outside rail – this will be the

Fitness and training
"I try to stay active doing whatever I can. Running, Ju Jitsu, swimming, paddle-boarding, mountain biking – whatever there is at that moment." – **Jay**

Fitness is vital. To be surfing fit is very different to any other kind of fitness. The universally accepted best training for surfing is swimming, the best being sea swimming. This is ideal in countries where the water is warm and safe, but impractical in colder climates. Swimming lengths and

Left & Opposite: Limbering up is a vital but often overlooked part of surfing. Being warm and loose can prevent injuries and allow for greater flexibility when attempting radical turns.

underwater in a pool is still good. It needs to be kept up for a long period of time because the results only show after committed training. But it is easily the best means of keeping super-fit and while swimming you are unlikely to damage muscles and joints.

And there is another reason a strong swimming ability is a prerequisite for anyone starting to surf. In surfing, it relates to self-preservation. A surfer's life in the ocean will entail numerous frightening and dangerous situations, so confidence in your water abilities is the backbone. You need to avoid panic and stay on top of it. To start with you should be comfortable swimming a good hundred yards in the open ocean, no problem.

On a more immediate level, another important part of preparation for surfing is the warm-up. Your muscles need to be loosened and stretched before the surf, and gently tweaked again afterwards. A good warm-up opportunity is the run down to the beach, or a quick cycle to the beach. If you drive there, a quick run up and down in your wetsuit, bouncing on the spot, swinging your arms or jogging on the spot are all good. Get some heavier breathing going and even a gentle sweat. Then stretch once you are warm.

From a physiotherapist's point of view, it's the stretching afterwards that is most important. It helps to alleviate minor soft tissue damage acquired during the surf, and serves to release tension and cramps that may result in stiff muscles. When stretching, it's not the number of stretches you perform, but the amount of time the stretch is held for. When stretching, it is of paramount importance never to push beyond a pain barrier if you feel one. These simple habits can help you surf better and for longer, but when all is said and done, the best training for surfing is surfing: time logged in the water is time spent getting fit.

Above: The balance board is an extremely useful aid in understanding the dynamics of weight distribution.

Dealing with crowds is an often overlooked aspect of modern surfing. With the frenzied surfing climate of today, along with the sport being so firmly enmeshed in the mainstream, the surf is often busy. We have to learn to deal with it and there are many ways of doing this.

Some people adopt the aggressor approach, and it enables them to get loads of waves at their home break. But if a guy is selfish and arrogant at his home break, he is not likely to get waves anywhere else. It's really a situation of give and take. Wait your turn, give a couple away. But when you decide on a wave make sure that your attempt is clearly marked, and paddle as if you are the only one paddling for it. Be prepared to pull back if someone inside of you takes off. You don't want to get in anyone's way.

After you've had a wave then wait for a while until your turn comes around again. No need to be selfish, no need to hassle. You can move around the break, sit further in or on a section where people keep falling, but don't paddle inside people who've been waiting for a while. Sometimes, when things get too crowded, it is better to go in and watch until the numbers drop. Keep an eye on the crowd movement. Sometimes, for no apparent reason, a large number of surfers will get out the water at the same time. This is a good time to paddle back out, and even if it does get crowded again, at least you had a chance to catch a few empty waves.

Crowds

"For a while I'd go out surfing and think, 'man, there's so many people out, this is so frustrating!' The frustration would overwhelm me and sometimes I'd just paddle in. I used to do that all the time and then I got to a point where I thought, you've gotta surf and they're gonna be out there no matter what. So now I don't let it worry me." – **Jay**

" sometimes, when things get too crowded, it is better to go in and watch "

Weather

Another key step to improving your surfing is learning to read the weather charts. In days past, predicting when the surf would be good was a mystical art. More recently it meant an intense study of the evening weather on the television, and then based on experience and foresight, a prediction could be made as to where the best waves would be the next day. But nowadays there is a plethora of surf sites on the internet, telephone prediction and update lines, paged reminders and a mushrooming surfcam industry. These days it is possible to plan a trip a few days ahead, and then fly half way around the world to meet up with a new swell. So learn your web addresses and your phone numbers, get into the loop because the information age is good for real surfers.

Opposite: When paddling out into a crowded situation, make sure that the surfer up and riding is aware of where you are.

Right: Crowds are an inherent part of today's surfing environment and need to be dealt with in an understanding manner. Violence doesn't solve anything.

6
soul surfing:
the blurring of the lines

"I think the best moment or day I have had surfing was the first day I actually got to surf Mavericks. I had been working on doing it for two years and when that day finally came I wanted it so bad. It was a dream come true for me. It was all I wanted in my surfing at that stage. After my first wave I had a grin from ear to ear and it lasted for weeks. Actually I think it's still there!" – **Jay**

Despite surfing being such a healthy, physical activity, non-surfers in the past saw surfers as typically young, idle people wasting their lives away. Lazing on the beaches and straying from the normal paths of education/job/family/retirement did not seem like a path towards fulfilment. It was only when the competitive side of surfing emerged that the world began to notice. It was

becoming a sport with an enormous following and the photos and films were ever more captivating. The mainstream, until then, had hardly noticed what a powerful, elemental activity it really was.

Surfing comes of age
Surfers slowly became established as real sportsmen – athletes striving for excellence and competitive highs. For a relatively low budget sport, larger and larger amounts of money began to pour in through prize money, sponsorship and commercialisation. Surf clubs flourished all around the world where people would pit their skills against each other. Although judging excellence in surf is extremely subjective, ways were found and standard methods became employed to find out who was the best.

Schools started leagues, the club scene mushroomed, and the professional side of surfing just kept on developing. A World Champion was crowned every year from 1976, and surf magazines abounded. Surfers wanted their shots in the mags so badly that often the simple ideals of surfing for fun and pleasure were all but left behind in the mad scramble for money, prizes and industry growth. Needless to say, with glory and financial reward on offer, some people were in surfing for all the wrong reasons.

Competitive surfing
The international professional circuit soon grew into a huge, multi-faceted juggernaut. Nowadays it encompasses the World Championship Tour (WCT), made up of the top 44 competitive surfers, and the World Qualifying Series (WQS); the lower rated pros striving to get into the WCT. There is a successful women's pro surfing circuit, which runs alongside and as a subsidiary of the WCT. There is the Longboard World Tour, the Junior League and the International Surfing Association Big Wave World Tour. This is over and above the packed amateur ranks of surfing in all

Opposite: Leaning into a big left at Pipeline, North Shore, Oahu, Hawaii.

Right: Contest hubbub – Hawaii.

countries around the world.
Some feel that competitive surfing had a price, and the price was surfing's soul. Surfing, they say, was led astray from its celebration of the environment, and the artistic perfection of expression.

"In 1995 my brother and my grandma died within a month. I broke up with my girlfriend of five years at the start of the 1996 Pro Tour season. It started out bad, and I was partying too much. Going into the Margaret River Masters in Western Australia my confidence and rhythm were shot. I somehow managed to win the event against a world-class field. All my friends from Santa Cruz were there and this was easily the biggest rush of my surfing career. This moment turned me around and I had my best years on tour after that."
– **Chris**

Wave pools now exist allowing contests to be held miles inland on man-made waves over a concrete bottom with fake shells littering an artificial sand beach. Film grips build camera cranes to hang over the waves and cameramen on dollies track alongside the breaking waves on perfectly

Left: Perfect trim.

Opposite: To the victor, the spoils. Chris with his trophies.

smooth surfaces to catch a new angle for TV channels worldwide. Some say it's not quite what the Duke had in mind. Yet while all this competitive growth continues to blow up, millions of other people are carrying on with the basic act of going surfing. These people cut a very different swath in the surfing community. Young and old, they have carried on surfing through it all for the simple joy and pleasure that it gives them. They are considered out-of-date by many, missing out on the booty available as clothing, sunglasses and wetsuit companies fight for their dollars and, they argue, for control of surfing's soul.

But this wasn't how it was supposed to be. Surfing as performed by the ancient Hawaiians was almost entirely for pleasure, and for healthy enjoyment. It was indulged in for the pure act of riding on a pulse of nature's energy, and the contentment this instils in the heart. This basic element of surfing is almost impossible to quash and as the industry and cash bonanzas have grown, more people have found it to be the reason they surf, not profit or fame.

Many people argue that competing is a good means of improving your surfing, and if you are successful, sponsorships can keep you surfing every day. This is surely what a soul surfer aspires to – surfing all day every day, getting in tune with the rhythm of the ocean finding the magic that only comes from spending time on the moving canvas.

The lines between soul surfing and surfing for fame and glory are becoming more and more blurred. With the unimaginable amounts of money involved in the sport, it has become a legitimate career option for many young people. This doesn't detract from their attitude to surfing and the art in their wave riding at all. These days it is generally agreed that the best surfer is always the one having the most fun.

The life span of a competitive surfer is fairly short compared to many other sports. A career will last ten years, maybe fifteen at most, on the cutting edge of competition. Then it's all over and surfing reverts back to a simple act of pleasure. Who is to say that a surfer with a free surfboard plastered with

"most surfers have soul, some just have more than others"

sponsors' stickers and wearing a pair of bright, new boardshorts for a photo session, has any less right to catch that one perfect tube? Does a feral surfer in a pair of well-worn boardshorts and a yellowing, sun-faded surfboard deserve it more? Surfing will look after itself. People who surf for the right reasons, who enjoy uncrowded waves and golden sunsets, who are prepared to get up in the morning when it is still dark and cold to get to a spot on sunrise and surf by themselves with just dolphins for company, they'll be looked after.

The longboard revolution

As the third or so generation of surfers came around, so the older guys, people who had lost their way either from work or families or moving away from the coast, wanted to get back into surfing. But surfing today on the modern, ultra-light equipment, is a labour intensive operation and a high level of fitness is required. So not surprisingly, the longer, cruisier boards of the 1960s came back into fashion, only this time with new materials and design advancements. To surf a longboard was no longer seen as out of date. In many situations it became the smartest option.

"I surf a longboard when the waves are smaller. I love surfing shortboards as well, but longboarding just seems to bring you to the roots of surfing. It's more of a playful, mellow attitude, which I really enjoy. Not that shortboarding isn't fun. It's just a different way of expressing yourself. There is a place for both. It is important to be versatile and be able to ride whatever board fits the conditions." **– Jay**

Longboards are easier to paddle, you can catch more waves on them, they float bigger people easily, and they bring to mind a forgotten era of surfing. At first there was much consternation among shortboard and competitive surfers, calling longboarders the older, unfit guys who were too busy in life to dedicate the time it takes to be fit and proficient 'real' surfer. But that didn't last long.

Left: I must go down to the sea again...

Opposite: ...to the lonely sea and the sky.

"Everybody seems to have their own opinion when it comes to the definition of a soul surfer. The cliché is the bearded vagabond with a clear board and black wetsuit, roaming the earth looking for uncrowded surf and cheap lobster. In contrast, as a professional surfer, I would be the clichéd anti-soul surfer, although personally, I can't think of anything more 'soul' than getting paid to surf the best waves on earth.

Some contest surfers lack soul but some of those 'soul surfers' are false. If you ask any surfer they will tell you they have soul. I think soul comes into it more when a surfer appreciates nature and the true gift of surfing. Much of the satisfaction comes not from a nice turn, but from the journey and the connection made with nature. Dolphins, whales, fish, birds, trees, reefs, sunsets – take these things away and you strip a perfect wave of its soul. Being a soul surfer is more a state of mind than a label. Most surfers have soul, some just have more than others..." – **Chris**

"the best surfer is always the one having the most fun"

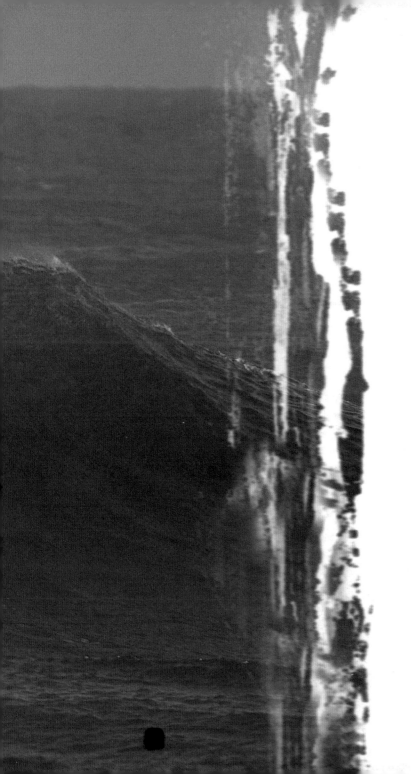

7
surfing
big waves

Below: Jay with his bigwave gun, and a smaller, slightly modified tow-in board.

Opposite: A mammoth wave.

"Big wave riding compared to normal surfing is a whole different thing. You have to be more focused and always thinking about it. Normal surfing isn't usually real dangerous, so you can do it more casually, but in big wave surfing the danger element is very clear and looks you in the face all the time. Because of that you always have to be in a different state of mind than normal. You always have to be ready for anything to happen. You must keep your mind clear and focused. Physically, mentally, emotionally, and spiritually you must stay strong. You also have to really love riding big waves and enjoy that state of mind to do it.

"I love riding larger waves which in turn means I like to ride big wave guns. Guns are a design combination of short and longboards. They have the rail length of a longboard, they're even sometimes a little longer, and they have the narrow outline of a shortboard. These boards are made to surf waves from fifteen feet to as big as it gets. This is usually the equipment I prefer.

"I had a wipe-out at Mavericks that was one of the craziest things ever to have happened to me. I paddled out to the line-up that morning all fired up and ready to catch whatever came my way. I saw that wave coming, looked at my line-ups, and decided to go. The winds were blowing really hard up the face of the wave and it wasn't letting me penetrate down the face, so I kept pushing hard trying to get into it. Finally it felt like I had it so I stood up and pushed on my front foot and tried to get down the face, but the wind was too strong and the wave was growing in size pulling me backwards up the face. Then all of a sudden I was looking down a four-story building of water with no bottom!

"The next instant I fell back into the lip. I just lay there trying to stay calm and in control of my head. Then the impact hit me and it felt like there was a cement truck dumping thousands of pounds of cement on me. It felt like my skin was being torn from my bones. Then I hit the bottom, which was good because it let me know which way up was. When I finally got to the surface there was already another wave there so I got a quick breath and went back under. After another wave I was able to swim over to the boat, get another board and go back out. I went back out and got eight more waves and made them all.

"That was probably the most scared I have ever been, but there have been a few other times which weren't far off." **– Jay**

Despite their passion, big wave surfers work on a different plane of consciousness. Not in a romantic sense – they actually do. Their brains work differently.

"big wave surfers work on a different plane of consciousness"

Millions of years of evolution have allowed the human race to devise a number of brilliant ways of eliminating danger. But now big wave surfers have gone full circle and started devising ways of inventing it. Sound weird? That's because it is. What's even weirder is the fact that fear is good for a human. A good dose of fear is soothing for the human psyche. When the brain detects danger, the human body sends out norepinephrine to every part of the body. Once this danger has passed, the body sends out dopamine to the brain, a pleasurable chemical, as a way to congratulate the brain for surviving. These chemicals are what make people want to surf big waves. It's a chemical addiction.

"My ideal surf day: the waves are twenty foot plus, and just the boys are in the water. Frosty, Peter Mel, Richard Schmidt, Jeff Clark, Grant Washburn, Evan Slater and a few others. The waves would be consistent and everyone is charging. Maybe an early session and a late session after going to breakfast at the Roadhouse Café with everyone else. Then ending the day after the second session by going to The Three Amigos for dinner on the way home. "– **Jay**

Down in Santa Cruz we have Mavericks, a famous big wave spot that was first discovered in 1962 by a group of surfers headed up by Alex Matienzo from San Francisco. Alex and his crew didn't actually ride any monster waves that day, just some small stuff. But Alex was so impressed with the place that he went ahead and named the spot after his dog Maverick, who wanted to paddle out, even though Alex and friends didn't. Some folks would argue over who claims the discovery of this place, but no one doubts that Jeff Clark is the master. For two

decades he surfed it virtually alone before he eventually told the surfing press. They soon ran pictures of it and projected Mavericks to the top of the list of the world's heaviest waves. Its position as a frightening beast was only underlined when a famous Hawaiian big wave surfer called Mark Foo was killed here in December 1994.

"To experience the ultimate thrill, you must be willing to pay the ultimate price." **– Mark Foo**

Foo lived in Hawaii where he served a long big wave apprenticeship at all the world's most famous spots. Compared to cold Northern California, Hawaii is a different story. Here the waves are big and the crowds are relentless. Surfers get forced to go for waves that otherwise might have been deemed too dangerous. The water is warmer and instils in some people a false sense of bravado. When there are legions of photographers on the beach and swimming in the water, one heroic wave can make a career, and some people do foolhardy things. Some get recognised for them, most just get wiped-out by the waves. Foo went through it all and along with a couple of others was regarded as an expert among the experts.

Opposite: A huge wave about to barrel over one lucky surfer at Pipeline, North Shore, Oahu, Hawaii.

Right: A lumbering beast of a wave at Sunset, North Shore, Oahu, Hawaii, with a lone surfer unloading a hard turn off the bottom.

Nowadays, about every second year, some major company comes up with a huge prize for the biggest wave surfed during that year. Sometimes there are limitations like the K2 contest in 1998/99, which offered a prize of $50,000 for the biggest wave paddled into without the aid of a tow-vehicle. This led to some crazy stuff. One Australian paddled out into Waimea Bay after the lifeguards had closed the beach. He had to be plucked from the jaws of death by a helicopter. He was after the money. In the year 2000 there was an even bigger prize on offer for the biggest wave caught, by any means. Does this mean that more people are going to be doing stupid things and put their lives at risk? Are they going to use up valuable lifeguard skills that could be better used elsewhere? Time will tell, but there's no doubt that since Mavericks was first surfed and Foo's attempts to surf the 'unridden realm', the meaning of 'big' has expanded.

Tow-in surfing

The new sport of tow-in surfing has also burst forward in the last decade. The media adores it. Some people think that this version isn't true to the roots of surfing. They argue that jetskis, or Personal Water Craft (PWCs), pollute the water and the air with fuel spilling into the ocean and smoky gas fumes. Another school of thought is that waves should be paddled into, and if they can't be, they shouldn't be ridden. In the tight circle of surfers at Mavericks, there is an unwritten rule that if someone wants to tow-in they have to have first made a name for themselves as paddle surfers at the break.

"I think tow-ins are great, as long as they are done right. They are great for allowing a surfer to get into a wave they could not physically paddle into. I don't think you should be doing them unless you are completely prepared for that kind of surf, and ready to deal with the situations you put yourself into." **– Jay**

"Surfing big waves is extremely empowering. I'm sure it's much like fire walking or bullfighting. To think that a human can have such control over the ocean and his emotions is truly amazing. Big wave surfing is not what it used to be. People like Peter Mel, Laird Hamilton and Jay Moriarity are taking it to cartoon levels. These guys are towing into waves that have a good chance of killing them if they make a mistake. This is now the definition of a big wave surfer – you basically have to be Evel Knievel on a surfboard. In the past a guy could rip Sunset Beach in Hawaii and be considered one of the elite. Nowadays Sunset is just a stepping stone to big wave stardom.

How far can it go? The biggest swells nature sends are now rideable. Maybe in the future they'll be doing three-sixties in 100ft tubes! I'm not counting out anything these days...." **– Chris**

8
surf travel

"The thing about the rat race is that even if you win, you're still a rat." **– Lily Tomlin**

To truly understand surfing and all that it stands for, one needs to get out and see how the spirit of surfing has evolved in different ways in other cultures. It is a huge reward in itself to experience the culture shocks, and to see where surfing fits into the scheme of things. To do this you need to travel.

For a surfer, a surf trip to a foreign shore is a voyage of discovery, a leap of faith, a journey of the mind as well as the body. It is during the loneliness of surfing far away places, where the spirit of nature is all around and the hardest choice is to decide between eating, sleeping and surfing, that one fully begins to understand the fire that rages in the belly of a dedicated surfer. It could be a trip to the jungles of East Java, perched on the edge of the ocean, in front of one of the most perfect, longest coral-reef waves in the world. It could be

among the hype and angst of the North Shore of Oahu, Hawaii, during the massive swells of winter.

Maybe in South Africa, shivering on the beach at Jeffrey's Bay, contemplating a paddle out into icy perfection, or the long, windy left-handers of Raglan, North Island, New Zealand. Maybe it's the cold and fierce waves of Ireland, or malaria-infested Lagundri Bay in Nias, off Sumatra. Travel is what keeps your surfing vibrant, what prevents it from being sucked too far into the modern world. Travel, despite its difficulties, high cost, hassles and negative apparent returns, is what keeps a surfer young and alive and in love with the life.

"The best place in the world for me would definitely be Alaska – for its pureness and untouched beauty. **– Jay**

"Travel is an evil mistress. She can bring you the ecstasy of perfect surf or the agony of $400 excess baggage fees and food poisoning. After ten years on the pro tour I've felt the extremes of both. Although, no matter how bad a trip got it almost always seemed worth it. There have been a few that I'd like to forget, but for the most part every journey had its charms and experiences – even if not for the surf or edible food.

Surfing and travel go together like milk and cereal. The best waves in the world are on tropical islands with diverse and interesting cultures. So you've got the most unique

spots in the world paired with some of the most exotic locations on earth – it can't get any better than that." **– Chris**

This is the reason why we put up with so much hardship and so many difficulties while lugging surfboards around the world. Those who have been to any of the beautiful, indescribable waves that fill this planet will know what we are here describing.

Surfers of the world unite

It's probably the same for sports all over the world, but sometimes it's odd to think that some little kid in Carlsbad, California is feeling the same little shiver of excitement, the same queasy little rush of butterflies as a grown man on, say, a beach in Bali. That the sight of a wave can touch the same emotional trigger in people of such vastly differing circumstances and culture is testament to surfing's universal appeal. It is a great leveller, for people of any age, sex or creed to enjoy.

In South Africa black and white surfers paddle out side by side. In Indonesia, Australians and Indonesians surf together in harmony. Hawaiians and mainland Americans share the same breaks in Hawaii. Australians share their beaches with the thousands of visiting British and Japanese surfers. The Japanese can be found surfing all over America. Like a huge, universal peace treaty, surfing has, with its own idiosyncratic style, paved the way for a form of world harmony.

The Holy Grail

One day, on your travels, you will arrive at a beach and all your perceptions and beliefs about perfect surf will be altered. There are so many nirvanas out there. Like love, perfection for a surfer is in the eye of the beholder. What is average for one surfer might bring another surfer to tears. Take Indonesia's Garajagan, formerly a secret known only by a handful of the best surfers in the world, now a destination which most surfers aim to visit at least once in their lives. These days there are camps there where you can stay, with numerous facilities available. But that doesn't mean the trip has lost its soul. Not everyone will see the beauty of living on the beach on the fringes of the East Javanese jungle, far away from civilisation and all mod cons. Around here the huts are on stilts to keep you away from the predators of the jungle – from tigers, poisonous snakes, scorpions, marauding wild boars and troops of hungry monkeys swinging in from the heart of the forest in search of food. The threats here are real, varied and truly wild. In the water there are sea snakes, burning corals, urchins and sharks. And the waves you surf break long and hard over a barely exposed, razor-sharp coral reef that can strip the skin off a surfer's back.

It might not be everyone's idea of fun. But for many surfers a trip to a place like Garajagan is a visit to the ultimate utopia. Part of the joy of surf travel is that it takes you away from the incessant buzzing of

Opposite: Surfboards waiting patiently.

Above: A palm-fringed beach on the edge of nowhere....Lagundri Bay, Nias, Sumatra, Indonesia.

modern life, from mobile phones, e-mails, deadlines and the pressures to make a buck, pay some bills and to buy more appliances. Out here on the perimeter it's not the same. Instead of stressing about parking and traffic, there is the worry of making sure you have enough mozzie cream on for the evening's onslaught, and whether there's a poisonous snake in your bed before you climb in it at night. When the waves go flat in a surf destination that doesn't have arcades or

shopping malls, there are other things to do. Have a long, precision shave. Mingle with the camp crew and learn a few phrases of their language. Watch them prepare an Indonesian meal. Catch up on some reading; try a few of the classics. Explore the coastline and the reef at low tide. Enjoy the sunset.

Think about it: How many equatorial sunsets will you actually get to enjoy during your lifetime?

Travel tips

Travelling with a surfboard can be a real pain, but it doesn't stop thousands of dedicated souls from trekking around the planet through some of the worst conditions you care to think of. Aeroplanes often charge for board carriage and the boards need to be packed well in a padded board bag. Road travel can be a nightmare in some countries where rules are slack and drivers always apparently in a hurry. Boat travel can range from perfect, smooth cruises to days adrift, storms and sinking ship nightmares. When you're not on the sort of journey a travel agent can plan, you're throwing yourself to the whims of life's wilder quarters and in many places this can be scary. But surfers still keep doing it. The draw is just too strong.

First aid and eco-travel

Aside from the ever possible great disasters, there is always the worry of minor injuries when you're on the road. All travelling surfers should carry a comprehensive first aid kit and have a more than scant knowledge of how to use it.

There are a few constant concerns when travelling to an equatorial destination. Quick action can prevent longer term damage.

Sunburn is one. A strong cream with a high Sun Protection Factor (SPF) is an absolute necessity. SPFs differ around the world – there is no universal rating system yet. A SPF 80 in the USA might not be as effective as a SPF 15 in Australia. Do some

research and even speak to a doctor or a dermatologist before leaving, especially if you have fair skin.

If someone gets bad sunstroke the most obvious immediate response is to get them out of the sun completely. Along with sunstroke there will be an accompanying degree of dehydration. This can be treated symptomatically. There are a number of different rehydrants available – they should be in the first aid kit.

Sunburn of the eyes can occur. This happens when the bright glare of overhead or dropping sun combines with reflections off the water. It is exacerbated by salt particles in the eye and can result in the retina being burned. Again, the immediate treatment is to get out of the sun. Apply eye-drops that remove irritation. Even sterilised water will help if the eyes are damaged. Stay in the shade or with sunnies on until the pain subsides (2-3 days.)

Stomach bugs are common. A pack of stomach antibiotics is good to have with you while on the road, as well as something for the runs. These are best reserved for emergencies, only then do they become imperative.

Then there is the ever-present danger of an injury off the reef. In warm water the chance of even a minor injury becoming horribly infected is very real. A good

disinfectant is vital, as well as an eradication disinfectant such as hydrogen peroxide. This will assist in the initial cleaning of a wound, and help loosen any particles of coral, as well as decrease the chance of initial infection. Cuts and abrasions need to be cleaned and treated a couple of times a day, otherwise the risk of infection is just too strong. If your wound does get infected, don't ignore it. Treat it well and avoid surfing and drinking alcohol. Antibiotic cream is a must for tropical travel.

Remember the constant threat of malaria. Cover up, burn mosquito coils, maintain a functional mosquito net. Take prophylactics. Find out what medication is needed for the area where you are going. Malaria is a constantly mutating virus and should be taken extremely seriously.

Finally, when camping out anywhere, it is important to be environmentally aware. Take trash away with you. Leave the camp cleaner than you found it. Bury your body waste deep underground and go far away from the camp. When tramping in a forest or jungle, try to stick to the footpaths, don't go bashing through the woods. Think about the people who will come after you, who also want to enjoy themselves.

Another joy of surf travel is that after everything it takes to get you there, no matter what the possible dangers are, when you're out in the water, it's just you,

your board and the waves. This is what it was all about in the first place.

Surfing, however and wherever you do it, is a celebration of life. It is an expression of feeling and emotion through a physical act, and it has the capacity to convert all those who come into contact with it.
So, if you're thinking about going surfing, don't think anymore. Get out there, now!

"the thing about the rat race is that even if you win you're still a rat"

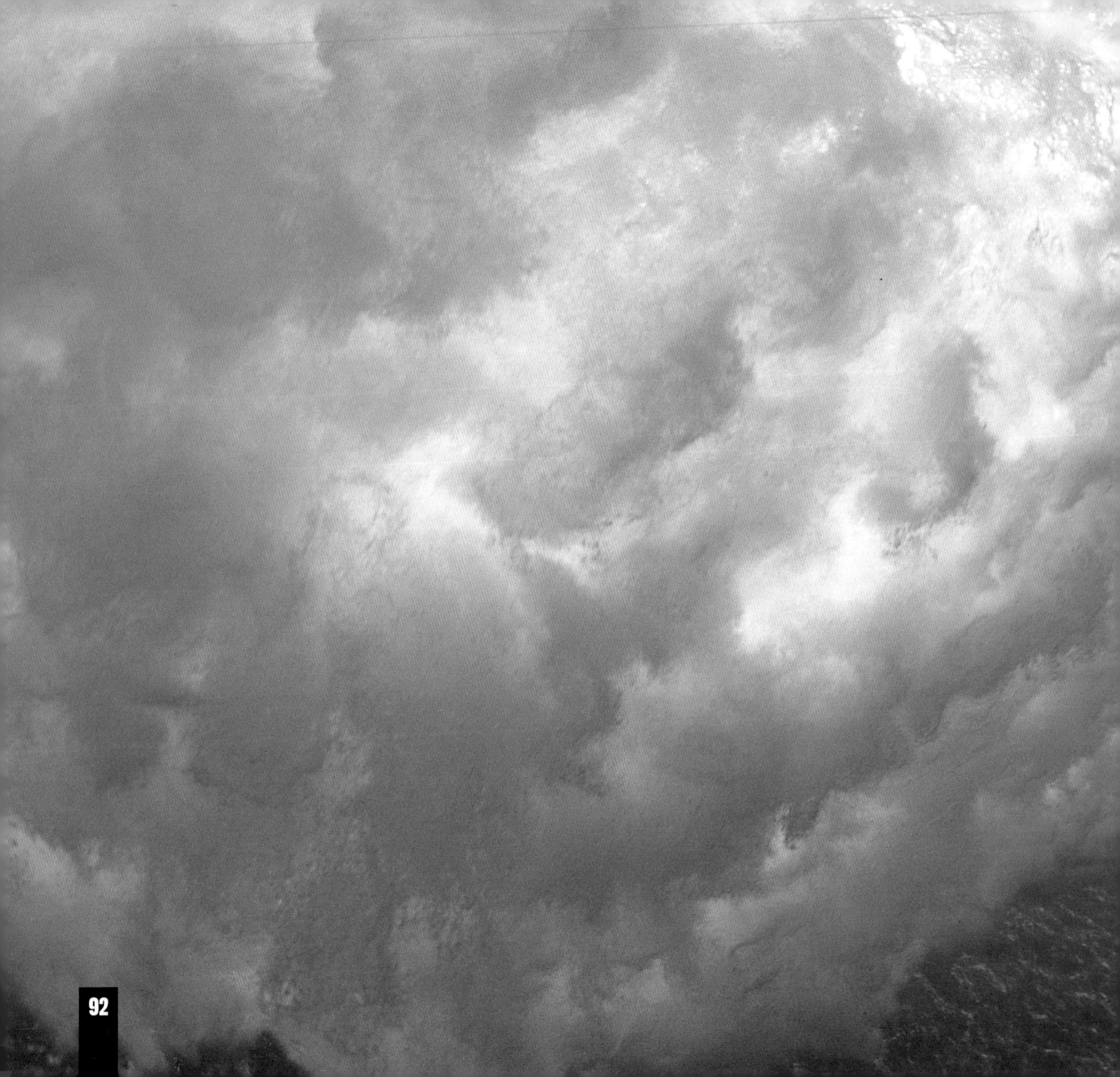

9
glossary

Aerial: An advanced turn when the surfer flies into the air off the back of a wave, then travels some distance in the air before landing back on the wave and continuing to ride it.

Backhand: When a surfer rides a wave with his/her back to it.

Barrel: A hollow part of the wave that allows the surfer to get inside while it is breaking.

Beachbreak: Waves that break over a sand bottom. Generally fairly gentle waves and more suited to beginners.

Body surfing: Surfing the waves without a board of any sort, using your body as a planing surface.

Bottom turn: A turn done off the bottom of a wave, usually after take-off.

Charging: To boldly surf big and powerful waves.

Clean: Good surfing conditions with just the right wind and swell combination or no wind at all.

Close-out: A wave that breaks all at once, in a long line.

Cross-current: A current that washes in a direction parallel to the shore-line.

Cutback: When the surfer turns back towards the pocket, or power-source of the wave.

Deck: The top of the surfboard. The surface that has wax on it and on which the surfer stands.

Double-up: When one wave catches up with another, resulting in a single wave with increased power.

Drop-in: When a surfer takes off on a wave that another surfer is already riding, the second surfer is dropping in on the first, who has right of way. This is not the right thing to do.

Duck-dive: A method of slipping under a broken wave while paddling out.

Face: The part of the wave ridden by a surfer – the unbroken part of the wave.

Floater: A manoeuvre when a surfer floats along the broken part of the wave or along the lip of a wave, before free-falling back into the wave and continuing with the ride.

Forehand: Surfing with your face to the wave.

Glassy: Surf conditions that are characterised by the complete absence of wind and a smooth shiny surface.

Goofy-footer: A surfer who surfs with a right foot forward stance.

Gun: A surfboard made for the purpose of riding big waves.

Hollow: A wave that breaks in a cylindrical shape as a result of shallow water and an offshore wind.

Leash: Urethane chord that attaches the board to a surfer's ankle by means of a Velcro clasp.

Left: A wave that breaks from left to right from the perspective of someone on the beach.

Line-up: The particular location where the waves usually break, where the surfers wait for waves to catch.

Lip: The leading edge of the breaking part of the wave, or the crest of the wave.

Longboard: Usually a surfboard over nine feet in length with a rounded nose. Ideal for beginners.

Mavericks: A notorious big wave spot in Half Moon Bay, North California, USA.

Nose: The front end of your surfboard.

Offshore: Used to describe conditions when the wind is blowing off the land and out to sea. Good for surfing.

Onshore: Wind blowing off the sea. Not good for surfing.

Pointbreak: Long, unvarying waves that usually break around a headland.

PWC: Personal water craft, jet skis or wetbikes. Used to tow surfers into massive waves and as a safety aid in big wave surfing events.

Quiver: A surfer's personal collection of surfboards.

Rail: The edge of your surfboard.

Reefbreak: A wave breaking over a rock or coral bottom. These waves can be dangerous.

Regular-footer: Surfer with a left foot forward stance.

Rhino-chaser: A long, sleek board designed for surfing very big waves.

Right: A wave that breaks from the right to the left, from the perspective of someone on the beach.

Rip currents: Also called rips. Currents that flow out to sea from an area into which waves have broken.

Sandbank: A formation of sand over which a beachbreak wave breaks.

Session: A period of time spent surfing.

Shorty: A wetsuit with short arms and short legs, used when the water isn't too cold.

Stall: To apply pressure to the back of your board in order to slow down. Usually in anticipation of a tube.

Stringer: The wooden piece running down the middle of your board, structured to give the board added strength.

Sunset Beach: A famous big wave spot on the North Shore of Oahu, Hawaii.

Tail: The back portion of your surfboard, characterised by a number of different outline shapes.

Tailslide: The result of weight being taken off the fins and allowing the tail to slide, mid-turn.

Three-sixty: Turning the board through three hundred and sixty degrees, either by spinning on the wave face or by carving off the lip.

Thruster: A surfboard with three fins. Made popular by the designs of Australian shaper, Simon Anderson.

Top turn: A turn off the top of the wave.

Tow-in: A modern phenomenon, when a surfer gets towed into a wave by a PWC because the waves are deemed too big to paddle into.

Traction pad: A pad of roughened material stuck onto the deck to prevent the surfer from slipping. Used instead of wax.

Tuberide: When a surfer rides inside a hollow wave. Possibly the sweetest moment in surfing, also possibly the most dangerous.

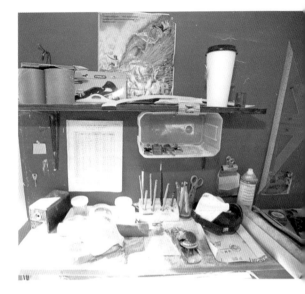

Waimea Bay: Famous big wave surf spot on the north shore of Oahu, Hawaii.

Wave pool: A pool that makes artificial waves by means of either a plunging or sweeping movement of the water.

Wax: Wax is rubbed onto the deck of a board to prevent the surfer from slipping.

Whitewater: That part of the wave that has already broken, the foamy part of the wave.

Wipe-out: To fall or to get knocked off your board.

WCT: World Championship Tour – the tour for the top 44 competitive surfers in the world.

WQS: World Qualifying Series – the secondary tour for surfers vying for the WCT.

Chilli is the global agency specialising in Freesports such as surfing.

Chilli provides services and products which include strategic consultancy, campaign implementation, event and TV production, media exploitation and design.

To find out more about the range of Freesports video titles available from Chilli visit chillivideo.com

For more information on Chilli please contact: info@chilli-news.com

Other titles available in this series:

The Ultimate Guide to Windsurfing
The Ultimate Guide to Mountain biking

Forthcoming titles from Chilli and HarperCollins*Publishers*:

The Ultimate Guide to Snowboarding
The Ultimate Guide to Skateboarding
The Ultimate Guide to In-line Skating